GREEN CLEANING 101

DIY Natural Cleaning Solutions with Vinegar and Other Frugal Resources That You Already Have

By
Sustainable Stevie

First Printing, 2012

ISBN-13: 978-1482085273

ISBN-10: 1482085275

Printed in the United States of America

Table of Contents

INTRODUCTION

Courtesy of Rubbermaid Products

I t's a given that popular cleaning products that you buy from the store are full of chemicals which means they are harmful to you, your family and your pets; not to mention the environment. Plus overall they're more expensive. Some of these substances include ammonia, chemically engineered perfumes, chlorine, dyes, phosphates, other solvents and neurotoxins. Sometimes just opening the container can give you a headache and cause nausea from the toxic fumes.

There's a delicate eco system here. When these chemical cleaning solutions have been used (sometimes all of it doesn't even get used), it's thrown into the trash which ends up in landfills thus polluting the soil and groundwater. This is harmful to living species because it eventually gets into their system.

So we'll take an alternative "natural" route that's safe, effective and have been around way before the 21st century! Most of the items listed below you probably already have in your home somewhere. And what's really nice is that they're affordable for most people. But you will be amazed at what they can do as far as cleaning is concerned.

It's been said that "natural" cleaning solutions are weak when it comes to doing a good cleaning, removing stains, etc. in comparisons to chemical commercial household cleaners. That's sometimes why people tend to shy away from eco-friendly products. If that describes how you feel, simply make your homemade cleaning solution a little more concentrated, and apply a little more manual scrubbing pressure. You'll be pleasantly surprised!

Listed below are 11 items we can use to make up our natural homemade cleaning concoctions and deodorizers for different parts of your home (bathroom, kitchen, bedroom, closet, living room, etc.). Interestingly, each item can be used in various other ways. But to keep it manageable, we will focus on their "cleaning" purposes.

Also, you'll find that some of the solutions overlap. In other words, if there's an ingredient you don't have readily available there might be another ingredient that you do have that can serve the same purpose. Let's break them down and have some fun with this!

SALT (aka SODIUM CHLORIDE)

(Most likely already have it at home or can buy it anywhere)

Salt is most commonly used as a food enhancer. But there's so much more to what it can be used for; especially for cleaning. It can be added with other natural cleaning ingredients or used alone to handle certain tasks.

5 Ways to use it for cleaning purposes

1. For removing coffee and tea stains from cups - dampen a cloth and sprinkle salt onto it and rub in circular motions.

2. As an ant deterrent - Make an unbroken path of salt across window frames and doorways. They wouldn't dare cross it! This might work for other little bugs too. Try it.

3. For polishing copper and silver - Make a thick paste with salt and vinegar. Apply the paste with a soft cloth onto your items. Then thoroughly rinse and dry them.

4. For removing that dull yellow look from white cotton and linen fabrics after you've had them for a while - boil them in salt and baking soda for an hour

5. For absorbing grease from pans - Sprinkle the grease with salt which absorbs it. Then wipe it. This will make it easier when it's time to wash it.

(WHITE) VINEGAR (aka IMPURE DILUTE ACETIC ACID)

(Can buy it anywhere)

Just by making a 50/50 solution of vinegar and water and putting it in a spray bottle, you'll have a natural, **all-purpose cleaner for countertops, stovetops, appliances, etc.** Vinegar is a primary ingredient for eco-friendly cleaning solutions considering it is a **deodorizer and disinfectant** which you'll see as you continue reading. It **removes soap scum, cleans shower doors and windows, cuts grease, clean linoleum and tile** (in most cases; test a little first).
CAUTION: Do not use vinegar on marble, no-wax floors, stones or hardwood floors (undiluted) as it is acidic.

1. Use undiluted, pure white vinegar to clean and remove the ring in toilet bowls - It works best if the water level is lower, so flush the toilet and then pour the vinegar all around the inside of the rim. If you want to thicken it, just sprinkle a little baking soda for extra cleaning power and then start scrubbing.

2. For laundry - Vinegar can also be used as a natural fabric softener by adding just a ½-cup in your rinsing cycle.

T I P ~3~

BAKING SODA (aka SODIUM BICARBONATE)

(Can buy it anywhere)

This is a mild abrasive and primary ingredient for eco-friendly **multipurpose cleaning**. It can be used as a **deodorizer** all by itself. It can also be used as a **carpet deodorizer, a copper and brass tarnish remover, scouring powder, silver cleaner, marble cleaner**, and many more uses.

1. For a carpet stain remover - Form a paste by mixing baking soda and white vinegar together. Use a small brush (maybe a toothbrush) and work the paste into the stain. Vacuum up the baking soda after it's thoroughly dry. Depending on how well it comes out, you might need to repeat this process on the stain.

2. For cleaning the drain of your sink - First, pour a ½ cup of baking soda down the drain. Second, pour a ½ cup of white vinegar. Third, for 15 minutes, leave it alone. And fourth, pour 2 quarts of boiling water to wash it down the drain.

TEA TREE OIL (aka MELALEUCA ALTERNIFOLIA OIL)

(Can buy it at any drug store in the pharmacy area and health food stores)

5 Ways to use it for cleaning purposes

1. Use as a shower, tub and tile cleaner.
2. Can be used as an antiseptic.
3. Add a small amount to laundry to remove musty, lingering odors
4. For mold and mildew control - Simply add 2 teaspoons of tea tree oil to 2 cups of water in a spray bottle. Shake well to blend. Spray your shower walls <u>without</u> rinsing. It usually takes a few days until the smell goes away. Its anti-fungal properties help to control mold and mildew.

If you spray the grout, the must and mold will be killed but the discoloration remains. It's the opposite of bleach in the sense that bleach removes the black mold color; but it doesn't kill the mold, which comes back. The tea tree oil kills the mold.

5. As a general purpose cleaner - Fill a 12 ounce spray bottle with warm distilled water. Add in 1 teaspoon of tea tree oil, 2 tablespoons of distilled white vinegar, and 1 teaspoon of Borax. Mix or shake it up until the Borax is fully dissolved. It also wipes out odor causing bacteria.

HYDROGEN PEROXIDE (aka H2o2)

(Can buy it anywhere - the traditional 3% solution is referred to here which is what is commonly sold)

10 Ways to use it for cleaning purposes

1.   All-purpose cleaner for tubs, sinks and countertops - Put a little on your cleaning cloth and wipe or spray the surface to kill germs and leave a refreshing scent.

2. Cleaning wooden cutting boards - Simply pour some on it to kill salmonella and other bacteria.

3. Cleaning toothbrushes - To kill germs, it must be soaked immediately after being poured from the bottle because H2o2 loses potency quickly after being exposed to light. No wonder it's packaged in dark bottles! Rinse it well before using your toothbrush again.

4. For a toilet or septic system disinfectant - In a dark spray bottle that filters out sunlight, fill a half with hydrogen peroxide and the other half with water. Spray some on the inside of the toilet bowl and let it stay for at least a few minutes then you can use a scrub brush to clean it. Your septic will not be damaged because the H2o2 will be diluted by the time you flush it. This is a great alternative instead of using bleach.

5. **For whitening laundry** - Instead of using bleach, add 1 cup of H2o2 to a load of laundry. Specifically to get blood out of the fabric, pour some directly on the spot and let it presoak for about 1 minute. Then rub that area and rinse with cold water. You can repeat the process if needed. Do not overdo it unless you want to ruin your fabric as H2o2 is a bleaching agent!

6. For mopping floors - Pour 1 gallon of hot water in a bucket along with a ½ cup of hydrogen peroxide.

7. **For cleaning mold and mildew** - In a dark spray bottle that filters out sunlight, fill 2/3 of it with water and the remaining 1/3 with H2o2. Spray the affected area and let it stay for a minimum of 10 minutes then wipe it off. In general, considering it's a bleaching agent, be mindful of what you use it on to preserve the colors of things.

8. **For cleaner dishes** - If you're hand washing, add a ½ cup to your sink's dish water.

9. **For a fruit and vegetable wash** - In a dark spray bottle that filters out sunlight, fill it with half water and half H2o2. Spray it thoroughly to kill bacteria and neutralize chemicals (especially if it was sprayed with pesticides which mean anything that's not organic) and rinse. To add longevity to your produce, do this right away when you get home.

10. For cleaning bacteria out of sponges - Pour half water and half hydrogen peroxide in a shallow dish. Soak the sponge in it for 10 minutes. Then thoroughly rinse it out and let it completely dry before the next use.

T I P ~6~

BORAX (aka SODIUM BORATE)

(Can buy it at hardware stores, some supermarkets, international grocery stores, or online. Commonly sold under the name **"20 Mule Team"**)

12 Ways it can be used

1. It has anti-microbial properties and can be used as a **disinfectant**. (There's no smell either.)
2. **Inhibits molds and fungal growth**
3. When combined with other cleaning products, it **enhances the cleaning power**.
4. Used for **cleaning carpet**; (but that's not the best time to have crawling babies and pets around)
5. **Can be used to clean surfaces, including chopping boards** - But wear gloves and rinse well when cleaning because it's strongly alkaline
6. **Kills cockroaches, ants, fleas** and other little insects; so don't inhale it!
7. **Good deterrent for mice** as they get bent out of shape when it touches their feet
8. **For sinks and drains** - Simply combine it with hot water

9. For getting rid of grease - Just add it to water along with liquid dish washing solution; rinse well

10. For cleaning windows, enamel surfaces and tiles - Add 1 tablespoon or a bit more to 2 or 3 liters of hot water depending on how grimy they are.

11. For cleaning ovens - Combine Borax, vinegar and baking soda into a paste. Take a brush to apply it throughout the oven. Let it sit there for at least several hours. Finally take a damp cloth to wipe it all off. Doing it this way totally spares you from those highly toxic commercial oven cleaners.

12. For boosting laundry detergent - Add a ½ cup to each wash load to remove soap residue from clothing, neutralize laundry odors, soften hard water, whiten whites and increase laundry detergents stain removal ability.

CAUTION: Don't mix it with or store it with acids. Keep it away from kids and pets.

You can take a look at Amazon to see Borax in its many forms here:

www.livesmartinfo.com/boraxproducts.

LEMONS / LEMON JUICE / LEMON ESSENTIAL OIL

(Can buy at the grocery store)

7 ways to use it for cleaning purposes

1. Use as a **disinfectant**
2. **Use to remove grease stains and mineral build-up** because of its acidity
3. Used as a **bleaching agent**
4. **For an all-purpose, naturally scented cleaner** - Combine the following into a spray bottle and shake it up: 3½ cups of hot water, ¼ cup of white vinegar, ¼ cup of dishwashing liquid, 2 teaspoons of Borax, and at least 6 drops of lemon essential oil.
5. **For deodorizing and cleaning garbage disposal** - Cut the peel off a lemon (or an orange peel can do the job too). Put it in the drain of your garbage disposal and let it run for 3 minutes. You'll be left with a fresh smell because it'll kill odor-causing bacteria and dissolve food build up.
6. **For wood furniture polish** - First wipe the furniture with a cloth to remove any excessive dust. In a spray bottle, combine a half cup of lemon juice with one cup of olive oil. Shake it up so that they blend together. Then spray a little on a cloth and

rub the furniture with it. Use a separate dry cloth to wipe it dry.

7. For removing rust - Make a paste with 50/50 lemon juice and Borax. Apply it directly onto the rust or submerge it into the solution. Let it sit for 25 to 30 minutes. Then use a damp cloth to wipe it off. But if you rinse it off, make sure to thoroughly dry it. You might need to do this process twice if you still see rust. Don't overdo it because you don't want to eat away the outer metal coating which would expose the underlying dull base metal.

T I P ~8~

RAW POTATOES

(Can buy at the grocery store)

How to use it for cleaning purposes

Remove rust from your cast iron cookware, baking pans, knives or other tools - Cut a russet or red potato either across in half or lengthwise, or just enough to where you can comfortably grip it. Dip the cut end in salt or baking soda and scrub the rusted area. If it gets slippery, thinly cut off the already used surface of the potato and repeat the same thing until the rust is gone. Then rinse and dry off.

T I P ~9~

BAMBOO CHARCOAL DEODORIZER (aka ACTIVATED CARBON)

(Can buy it online)

What it is used for

It's extremely porous and can be used as a general **deodorizer to absorb moister, smells and lingering or foul odors** in refrigerators, freezers, closets, drawers, cupboards, shoe areas, under the kitchen sink, bathrooms; litter boxes, just about anywhere; including your car. It's non-toxic and environmentally safe. Some prefer it over baking soda.

What forms it comes in

The size, shape and containers of it depend on where you want to place it to refresh the air. For example, the **bamboo charcoal deodorizer** comes in a pouch and there are different pouch sizes. It is the most popular. There's a **powder** kind that can be turned into a thick cleaning agent and also a **mud that can deodorize toilet bowls** up to 6 months. This is definitely worth looking into further as not enough people are aware of how wonderful this is. If you would like to see the various forms it's packaged in at Amazon, take a look here: www.livesmartinfo.com/bamboocharcoaldeodorizers

RUBBING ALCOHOL (aka ISOPROPYL ALCOHOL)

(Flammable and not to drink - Can buy it anywhere)

11 ways to use it for cleaning purposes

1.   For Cleaning chrome - Take a soft, absorbent cloth and pour some rubbing alcohol onto it. Wipe the chrome and no rinsing is necessary. It'll kill the germs and evaporate.

2.   Cleaning venetian blind slats - Get a flat tool such as a 6-inch drywall knife or spatula and wrap it in cloth. Put a rubber band around it to secure it. Simply dip it in rubbing alcohol and start cleaning away.

3.   To prevent window frosting during winter - Wash your windows with one quart of water and a ½ cup of rubbing alcohol. After washing, use newspaper to polish it for a shine.

4.   To remove hair spray from mirrors - Those hair spray spots are stubborn! Clean your mirrors with rubbing alcohol and it'll remove the sticky residue.

5.   Getting rid of fruit flies - Fill a spray bottle with rubbing alcohol. As the annoying little gnats are flying around, spray them to drop dead. It's not as strong as a commercial insecticide; but it's more eco-friendly.

6.   Removing ink stains - Presoak the spot(s) for a few minutes in rubbing alcohol just before laundering.

7.   For preventing neck stain around the collar - Wipe your neck with rubbing alcohol before getting dressed and it'll help prevent that ring around the collar of your clothing.

8.   For cleaning the phone - Wipe your phone down with rubbing alcohol to both disinfect it and cut through the grime.

9.   To remove permanent marker stains from countertops - Most countertops are made from non-permeable material such as plastic laminate or perhaps marble. Use rubbing alcohol to dissolve marker stains back to a liquid state and then simply wipe it off.

10.   For removing dog ticks - Dab the leech with rubbing alcohol which causes it to loosen its grip. Then grab it as close to the dog's skin as possible to pull it straight out. To disinfect that area, simply dab it again with rubbing alcohol.

11.   For dissolving windshield frost - Fill a spray bottle with rubbing alcohol and spray the car glass. Instead of scraping, simply wipe the frost off easily.

T I P ~11~

OLIVE OIL

(Can buy at the grocery store)

5 ways to use it for cleaning purposes

1. To help prevent wicker furniture from cracking - Use a soft cloth to gently rub the oil into it. Warming the olive oil works better.

2. Remove scratches from leather (furniture, jackets, etc.) - Pour just a dab onto a cotton cleaning cloth and in a circular motion lightly rub it into the scratch.

3. Get paint off your hands - Rub some into your skin where the paint is and leave it there for 5 minutes then thoroughly wash your hands with soap.

4. Use as a door hinge lubrication - Gets rid of the squealing sound.

5. For polishing wood furniture - Mix together 2 cups of olive oil and 1 cup of either lemon juice or vinegar. Dip a soft cloth into the solution and rub it into the furniture. To get out scratches, make the solution 50/50 which means if you use 1 cup of olive oil, also use 1 cup of either lemon juice or vinegar. Combine them together and rub out the scratch.

8 HELPFUL CLEANING AIDS

1. Spray bottle - Keep in mind not to reuse spray bottles that have contained other chemicals.

2. Squeegee - A great tool to use when cleaning windows.

3. Cleaning rag or cloth - There's no need to go out and buy this. Just use an old piece of 100% cotton clothing that you no longer wear; but cut out the zipper or cut off the buttons. You can even use old towels or worn out bed sheets which you can cut into different sizes if you want.

4. Natural sponges - Great for cleaning stains off carpets.

5. Microfiber cloth - Its fibers are made of nylon and polyester that's finely split and woven into soft, absorbent, and thin material. Because it is electrostatic, dust naturally attracts to it. The fibers absorbs dirt and oil and does not shed lint like other cloths and paper towels; which makes it easier to clean mirrors with no streaking either. Interestingly, it can repel water; yet when dampened with hot water, it's great for cleaning window frames, walls and countertops without cleaning solution. They cost a little more but last longer because you can wash and reuse them. And they dry really fast too. You should be able to find these around at drugstores or car accessories stores. But you can definitely find them online. If you want to see what they look like, you can see it at Amazon here: www.livesmartinfo.com/microfibercloth.

6.   Scrub brush (soft and firm bristles) - Some brush bristles are firmer for hard scrubbing that doesn't damage the article. But soft bristles are for more delicate items that still need a scrub. You can also use a toothbrush if that's more suitable for what you are cleaning.

7.   Razorblade - Makes it easy to scrape off dried and stuck-on things from mirrors.

8.   Newspaper - Instead of paper towels, newspapers are great for wiping windows and mirrors.

Granted, some people are not into measuring things and mixing cleaning solutions. That's fine. This is where you can alternatively go to the health food store, hardware store, grocery store or online and buy "natural" cleaning products that's already mixed with these same natural ingredients. These are becoming more available now because companies are feeling the pressure to become more eco-friendly, safer and less toxic.

It's nice to know there are so many other less costly options available for cleaning that we can all take advantage of and thus contribute to a safer environment for the planet.

RESOURCES

- http://chemistry.about.com/od/chemicaldata bases/a/Chemical-Names-Of-Common-Substances.htm
- http://chemistry.about.com/od/howthingswo rkfaqs/a/howboraxworks.htm
- http://www.greenfootsteps.com/borax-information.html#anchor-name
- http://www.teatreewonders.com/household-cleaning-products.html#
- http://www.truthorfiction.com/rumors/h/hy drogen-peroxide.htm
- http://www.ecologycenter.org/factsheets/clea ning.html
- http://en.wikipedia.org/wiki/Activated_carbo n
- http://www.dailygrommet.com/products/253 -ever-bamboo-charcoal-deodorizer-for-closets-shoes-rooms-all-natural

Printed in Great Britain
by Amazon